MW00366986

FINISHING LINE PRESS

www.finishinglinepress.com

SNOWBIRD

poems by

Iris Litt

Finishing Line Press
Georgetown, Kentucky

SNOWBIRD

Copyright © 2017 by Iris Litt
ISBN 978-1-63534-097-6 First Edition
All rights reserved under International and Pan-American Copyright Conventions.
No part of this book may be reproduced in any manner whatsoever without written
permission from the publisher, except in the case of brief quotations embodied in critical
articles and reviews.

ACKNOWLEDGMENTS

Bayou Mirror: *The Bryant Literary Review*
The Arm: *A Slant of Light*, a Codhill Press Anthology
Sundreamer: *DeKalb Literary Journal*
House of Towels, Gentrification Song: *The Avatar Review*

Publisher: Leah Maines

Editor: Christen Kincaid

Photo of pier on cover: Marcia Haley

Author Photo: Iris Litt

Cover Design: Iris Litt and Phillip Levine

Printed in the USA on acid-free paper.
Order online: www.finishinglinepress.com
                also available on amazon.com

Author inquiries and mail orders:
Finishing Line Press
P. O. Box 1626
Georgetown, Kentucky 40324
U. S. A.

Table of Contents

Section 1: Downsouth

Bayou Mirror

At first on the island
I gushed my amazement
at this mirror of a bayou

delaying the day
when I would have to acknowledge:
high tides don't wash happiness ashore
seabirds are diving for food not fun.

Everything reflected in the bayou is real:
the house with the barking dog
the house with the quarrelling couple
the dying tree

but reality can't erase beauty

and nature is still innocent
like a beautiful young woman with no mirror
so she doesn't know she's beautiful.

The Florida House

Of all the boxy little Florida houses
the broker showed me, this was the best.
I don't exactly mean the house itself;
it was the owner, or rather his ghost
not that he was necessarily dead
but the broker said they took him away
suddenly one day. The ambulance came
and he didn't come back,
maybe he's in a home
thinking of this house, his real home.
But it was his desk that got to me the most
with an Unfiled Pile like mine
and so many of my books on his shelves
and some of the same kitchen dishes
and the prized tree out in front,
not a palm, more a northern tree.
I could get up in the morning
and walk out and stand under the tree
and go back to the desk.
So maybe when the broker told me what happened to him
or, for that matter, to millions of others
it wasn't so much his tragedy,
this everyday so-what-else-is-new tragedy,
no, it was this:
because of his house,
he was I and I was he.

Windsounds

Out here the island is so narrow
it's almost like a ship
and some nights the wind
sweeps across from gulf to bay
and has found some kind of tunnel
in our carelessly built Florida house
that turns its song to a moan
which sounds to me cold and mournful and alone.

I'd expect it on Nantucket
or Cornwall or the moors
where Cathy cried out his name
and sent her voice to Heathcliff on the wind

but not on our island of friendly breezes,
not after a day of island sun

so now I see the wind—
like the seabirds, the seagrapes, the mangroves,
the bayous, the seawall and all—
yes, I still see the wind
as friend.

The Wind Tunnel

The wind has found
some kind of space
a wind tunnel, they call it
that changes its sound
in this island place.

At first I thought a thoughtless neighbor
had moved in and played music all night

and I even stepped outside
in my pink cotton nightshirt
to try to define that sound
and saw the palms bending forward
and waving their green hair in the wind

but there was no new neighbor
no reason for anger
since I found
it's just wind
and wind is wind
so I don't mind.

Happy Hour

Shirley, the huge green leaves are luxuriant this year
the palms healthy, the sun bright
on white clapboard and amber stucco
and it is five o'clock everywhere and
on the old pier the music and wine
and laughter are flowing.
This is not a grief poem, a missing-you poem
which would be more about me than you.
This is about you and our island
and the leaves and the sun
and the seawind and the endless horizon.
This is about you, who are missing it,
not about me missing you.

It's Happy Hour now
and we're all still chasing happiness
while happily settling for the sting of the wine,
the sun on the bay, the fun,
just fun and to hell with happiness.
Such as it is, this is the life
you've lost, goodbye, Shirley, goodbye.

Packing for Florida

My clothes are vying for the chance
to come with me.
They will be crowded together
in the baggage hold,
bumpy boring cold.

Now stacked on my mother's Victorian couch
against the tapestry of red and gold and cream
they watch me like refugees in Rwanda
whose lives depend on being chosen.
I tell them there is not room for them all
and only certain kinds of clothes
can come with me to the sun
while outside the big window behind them
huge chunks of snow begin to fall.

Black Sweatshirt

When I saw the black sweatshirt
at the Roser Church Thrift Shop
I thought, A black sweatshirt,
well, I don't know about that,
maybe for the city
but not for this sun and sea

yet it fit perfectly and was soft as
we persist in thinking a cloud would be
and did I tell you the price: two bucks.

Cut to the little house with palm trees
where we all curse the weathergods
if it's sweatshirt weather at all

but I say to my black sweatshirt
Thank you for showing up
and it says with feigned nonchalance
oh, my pleasure, I'm glad you bought me
and I will keep you warm and happy
when that stubborn untropical wind
blows in from the sea.

Fish Dinner

Always the caught fish
flopping on the dock,
desperate, uncomprehending eyes,
fate sealed, no way out,
gasping the next-to-last breath
finally the last

and around them the happy children
running on the beach
the vacationing parents
on their outdoor barstools,
the deadly, focused fishermen

all contemplating their fish dinner.

House of Towels

We've always made houses out of
what happens to be around.
Sod, hay, ice, desert sand,
sticks and stones, roofs of palm frond.
And when I went to visit her
in that place, all I saw
at first was a heap of white towels,
waiting for the wash, I thought

and then I knew she was in there,
had built her house of the one natural material
indigenous to this place, and moved in for good.
The huge towels were wrapped and re-wrapped
around her, but most distinctive was the hood,
a monk's cloak, medieval in subtropical Florida,
craftily draped so the front
could open or close in the middle.
She always had an inventive mind.

I parted the white hood in the middle
and saw her face, smaller, wrinkled, a shrunken head
and said, Hi, it's me, it's I, remember me?

but she had taken the monk's vow of silence
and all I could say was, I miss you,
I love you, I'll think of you
and finally she said very faintly, Thank you
and I closed the door to her white house.

Anger Management in Florida

No anger here: the gulls
don't ask themselves Why fly?
or if it's fair that there are fewer fish.
The bayou gleams in the sun;
although polluted, it will still hold your kayak.
Someone did something to me
I'd never do to them
but it's simple here:
I go out on the dock of the bayou.
The palms, the birds, the tides are all doing their thing
and I watch worse things happening to them
than what happened to me:
the fish is eaten, that egret has a hook
in its jaw, it can't eat,
it will die, now why
did this happen to this particular bird, yet I'll bet
he's not thinking, Why me?
Me, myself, moi, who am I
to expect kind treatment forever?
Here beside the bayou,
 forgetting who schemed against me
I humbly take my place
in this gorgeous scheme of things.

Florida News

The garbage hasn't been picked up;
they keep saying "soon".
It smells awful and there's a raccoon
living in there, sharp teeth, crazy eyes.
The landlord hasn't fixed the door lock,
the broadband doesn't work

so I pick up the local paper.
A young mother was kidnapped
while her two babies slept,
a pile-up on Route Four killed ten people,
a pretty little nine-year old girl was taken from her bed
in the trailer park and she's dead.

I thank the tabloid for this news,
which puts my life in perspective. I can choose
not to worry, while they look
into a gun barrel or a fire or struggle for breath.
I used to scorn the Daily News but no more. I thank it kindly
and go on cheerfully to mop the kitchen floor.

Straight Streets

They grew from the paths between the crops

on land as flat as a plate

land my mountain mind named bland

except that it's edged with the sea

a sea flat, too, but changing, changing

from white-etched steel

to sunspark and glow,

the Gulf of Mexico.

The farms, gone

strawberries gone, lettuce gone

the sandy paths now straight streets

someone planted houses

so only houses grow.

Sundreamer

Stoop step and wall sitter
heathen hoyden
public apple-eater peanutcruncher seedmuncher
parkluncher statue-leaner sundreamer
how did you get so far north
so direction-scattered so far from
what matters?

Homemaker in cafés
parks plazas piazzas place's and plati's
there where the weathergods are severe
and their congregation scurries
canvassing for nuts
to amass in frozen trees

come to where we splash bare
as dolphins and pair natural fierce and loyal
as pigeons in the square
and care like children

because now you are so south warm right
come play with us
and come to stay
in this lovely new hemisphere.

The Snowbird Returns

An unremarkable evening, March-cold
yet with a hint of spring that may be only in the mind
light till 6:30, unlike the December day I left
dark at five. Now the land
exhausted from winter, is dressed in drab:
a camouflage pattern
of brown, tan, a trim of evergreen
the deer tan, the squirrels grey, the bears
still sleeping

and the mountain still shrugs its huge shoulder
and the land rustles a bit in the wind and waits.

It's an unremarkable evening but what's remarkable
is that I am here again.
The plane flew smoothly and landed smoothly,
the road home clear and winding and untrafficked,
the house clean and peaceful not even complaining
about its three-month wait.

I close my eyes and brilliance reappears:
the sky, the palms, the mangroves, the bayous
and the tall white heron. I open my eyes
and the brown mountain stares back

and I love it all the more for enduring this winter
and I know I'm as rooted as the mountain
and I know I'm home.

Section 2: Upnorth

Snow In the Country

Snow, which is supposed to hide, reveals
the bootmarks in my woods
and tiretracks which, like fingerprints,
can be examined by the curious one.
Snow in its phony white innocence
serves loud testimony in this incredible silence.

Whereas summergrass cooperates,
bounces back conspiratorially after walkers,
snow in its alleged peace
squats on my land and, in ungrateful betrayal,
shouts of the inevitable unpeace of my life:
the friends who've fled to the central heating
of cities and tropical suns,
and the one who stayed
yet examines the tracks of the suspected ones

until I, at the manypaned window
by the voracious woodstove, ask:
In this deep mountain winter with its hundred snows
does it matter who comes and goes?

Message to One Wooded Acre

How can this puffed-up document say
I own a waterfall, a bird, a tree, rights to sky?
It does and, noblesse obliging, I
study you like a person, play god-of-the-land
learn your streampatterns, shape and shade of wood,
trees that die but still stand, language of
squawks, grunts, chirps, buzzes, tenant voices
little different from those of hindleg walkers
trying to make themselves understood.

I watch eggs hatch
and all kinds of babies grow
as mine did, am doctor to broken wings,
rescuer to orphans in snow
yet, when angered, attack raccoons
who stage garbage raids, catch
moths and am murderer to ants and mice.
I watch them from behind glass
and praise us for building in this wilderness
this warm, dry structure of siding, tarpaper and shingle
with its technology of duct tape, hooks and eyes
but take it all back and become another huddled ant
when lightning sends a tree just-missing my roof.

As my tenants scurry away,
slither under rocks, curl into treetrunks, burrow into soft sod
I, having caught that storm's eye, am my non-god self
more helpless and huddled than they, and
hearing no voices talking back from that forest to thunder and rain,
like them, I bow to the power of the sky.

The Tyranny of Summer

The clouds of fall have come
to release me from the coercion of the sun
and from the greens and blues that pull me out the door
belittle my earnest desk
seduce me down the pinecone path
with birdsong and leafrustle.

I've called myself a tropical flower
grinning from behind the brilliance of elephant leaves
but I'm northern, too
enticed by steely clouds and bare branches
happy when the pale, shrinking sun says
go on inside, go do your work
and stop your malingering,
I'll see you in spring.

Gentrification Song

Now I praise all leaning picket fences
with at least one spoke missing
all trailers zoned to the fringes of town
all rutted dirtroads all farmhouses morphed to
rooming houses with signs plastered
in the entranceway all shabby RV's
that someone is obviously living in
and the woodstove the chamberpot the nine-foot hand-dug well

and all my memories of rural life

only the memories aren't shabby
but bright with autumn reds
radiant with yellows and sunset pinks.

Oh I know I'm glorifying that time:
We got ready for bed at the local coffeeshop
where the water was running and warm
(we said elegantly, which restaurant shall we
get ready for bed in tonight?)

and we lugged water bottles in the car
thinking of all the people who lugged water without cars.
We tried putting the water bottles on our heads like in Africa
and collapsed laughing,
then we put them on yokes across our shoulders
and got bursitis.

Now we have sleek cars and central heating
and hot baths in warm rooms

but I'm glad the mountain looks the same
though more pockmarked with houses
and the crows are still raucous.

I Am Making a Place

I am making a place for myself in the woods by the stream
I am raking a path from the road through the woods to the stream
where the stream levels out for a while across the road
on its path from high on the mountain to the town in the hollow below

I will sit on a log in the place I am making and watch the sun
playfully touching the treetops and then moving on
and listen to birds conversing across the high trees

the place in the woods I am making is only for me
my place in the wildness that is not really wild any more
just a clearing in the woods by a stream that runs down to a town
as people have always made clearings to place themselves in
where the stream is your music and the sun is your light
and the forest creatures your company

and of course I am grateful for the house across the road
on the land someone cleared, my shelter from rain, heat and cold
like the nest of the bird and the cave of the bear
and the burrow of the woodchuck and the thicket of the deer

so the place I am making in the woods across the road by the stream
is also my home, my natural home.

The Orange Stanchion

Nothing I see from the window
is manmade except the road,
dirt when I came here, now paved
and widened, even-sided except where I swept
the still-wet shale at the sides of my land
back onto the road as though to reject the paving
so now this road's got scalloped edges.
Dust no longer rises when one of those too-fast pickups goes by,
yes, the road is manmade but by now
it's just part of the green/brown landscape
just branches and bushes climbing
the high trees to the sky
green vertical carpet so thick it's a bit too dark
except at noon in our clearing,
well, as I was saying, nothing manmade
except for that orange stanchion.
The men came one day in their
matching orange vests and plunked it down
at road's edge where a fallen tree sticks out
just about six inches too far
and then I guess they forgot it.
It's like a painting, all that green and brown
and then the bright orange cone
standing alone, defiant, brilliant and unignorable
reflecting the sunlight, shining through mist,
as though it wants to say
the humans are here
and aren't going away.

The Dog and the Stream

When my neighbor told me
that his sweet dog
was seriously sick, I was sad, very sad

but when he told me
he takes her to the stream
that runs through my land
and she gratefully lies down
as the rushing water soothes the itch and pain

I moved beyond sadness. Something about
how the stream washes away all pain

and I pictured her dog dream:
the stream, cool against her hot skin,
carries her to a dog heaven where she can
romp eternally with her kind and devoted friend
and catch the frisbee again.

The Annuals

They've had their year.
I've watered them
fed them
talked to them

and in return they were
simply there
each morning when
I opened the door to gauge
the temperature of the air.
With the help of the breeze
they waved hello
from their redwood box
in red and pink and yellow
and white and vivid green.

A year for them
a hundred, maybe, for me
it's all the same.
How long is not the test
but how much:
how much we were beautiful and free.

It's the first frost morning
of the year.
All I can say for them
and all of us:
I hope they were happy here.

The Arm

I was going to get up early
and make a Things To Do list
when your sleepy arm landed
around my waist, your hand in my hand.
The digital clock said 5:30am, your arm
went first on top of the covers, I picked it up
and put it undercover for two good reasons,
your arm would be cold in the country dawn
but the real reason was simple,
your skin against mine in sleep. That's all:
your bare arm around my bare waist.
And outside our window, the cry of the crow.
the lighting of the sky. the sound
of the stream rolling down the mountain.
We are bears in our cave, we are deer
warming ourselves on each other.
We are part of a picture, pieces in a puzzle,
notes in a rhythm. We turn, the earth turns,
we sigh and sleep.

Neighbor, Greenwich Village

You know that person is there.
You just know he/she is there.
You're walking by, the light is on
the TV reflects in the mirror
and you look for the actual neighbor
ah, there at the edge of the kitchen
a flutter of apron against
the white of the fridge
and beyond the door, the bed
and you think of them sinking their heads
into the pillow and watching TV
soon, soon, as the late dogwalkers trot home
and the silence in the street brings sleep
and they sleep so now you too
can lock your door
and read the mail and sleep.

The neighbor is moving July first.
She sends a card with the new address
three states away: "The chowder pot
is always on"; they'll be there
but they won't be here

like the artifact that has been
on your mantel all your adult life
just here whether or not you use it.

The River Remembers
(After Hurricane Sandy)

I remember my girth
my enormous freedom
the bare feet
along my shore

and when that trail
became Greenwich Street
and the settlement Greenwich Village
and the feet wore boots
and the ones who wore boots
dumped everything into me
and named it landfill
though it should have been riverfill
and on it, on <u>me</u>, they built
their red brick rowhouses

I scrunched my broad shoulders
shrugged it off you might say
and stayed within my banks.

Now they're saying that I flooded
wherever there was landfill.
Yes, I did.
When the hurricane came
I made my move, moved instantly back
into my domain,
took back what was mine.
Let them think that the river forgets.
I'll do it again
but I mean no harm.
I am only reclaiming my own.

Writing Checks After Death

The guy in charge of the cemetery
thought I would like this site.
It has a seasonal view, Mead's Mountain in winter
and you can hear the stream year round.
We laughed because we were living proof
that most people can't imagine being all dead,
I mean, really thoroughly totally dead.
So I wrote him a check for $700,
my rent for eternity.
Yes, I like it here
and I don't have to write any more checks.
But as you can see, I refuse to stop
writing poems.

Iris Litt is the author of two previous books of poetry: WHAT I WANTED TO SAY from Shivastan Publishing. and WORD LOVE from Cosmic Trend Publications. She has had poems, short stories and essays in many magazines and anthologies, including the SATURDAY EVENING POST, CONFRONTATION, THE WIDOW'S HANDBOOK, BRYANT LITERARY REVIEW, PINYON, THE NEW RENAISSANCE, THE RAMBUNCTIOUS REVIEW, SCHOLASTIC, ATLANTIC MONTHLY (special college edition), TRAVELLERS TALES, PACIFIC COAST JOURNAL, WRITER'S DIGEST, THE WRITER and others. She leads writing workshops in Woodstock, NY and has taught creative writing at SUNY/Ulster, Bard College, New York Public Library, and many other venues in New York City and the Hudson Valley. She lives in Woodstock, N.Y. and New York City's Greenwich Village and winters on Anna Maria Island, Florida, the inspiration for SNOWBIRD.